S.T.A.R.

JUNIOR
FIRST
AID

About the Author

Sheila Greeley is an R.N., as well as a C.P.R. and First Aid Instructor. She has been working as a staff nurse in surgery at Peninsula Hospital for 20 years. During the last 10 years she has also been teaching emergency care courses to both adults and children throughout San Mateo County. Sheila is married and has 2 children.

For information about copies
of this book write to:

F.A.C.T.
Sheila Greeley, R.N.
211 Trysail Court
Foster City, CA 94404

Illustrator

Susan Strong
San Mateo, CA

S.T.A.R.

JUNIOR
FIRST
AID

An Easy-To-Read
Manual For Children
And Adults

by
Sheila Greeley, R.N.
C.P.R. and First Aid Instructor

illustrated by
Susan Strong

ISBN: 0-936029-19-6
Library of Congress Catalog Number: 89-51922

Copyright - 1987, 1989 Sheila Greeley
Revised Edition: 1992.

Manufactured in the United States of America
By Western Book/Journal Press
San Mateo, California 94402

Library of Congress Cataloging-in-Publication
    Greeley, Sheila
    Star/Junior First Aid

DEDICATION

"S.T.A.R." JUNIOR FIRST AID is dedicated to my children, Ryan and Brandon, and is written as a tribute to children everywhere who have the desire and ability to help people in need.

ACKNOWLEDGEMENT

I wish to acknowledge the following organizations for their resource materials:

San Francisco Bay Area Regional Poison Control Center
Pacific Bell
Pacific Gas and Electric
American Red Cross
Alisa Ann Ruch California Burn Foundation

Technical review and advice were provided by:

Robert Arrick, D.M.D., President, Professional Dental Group, San Diego, California; President, Doctors on Call, Inc., Portsmouth, Rhode Island.

Allan Braslow, Ph.D., Faculty, National Conference on Cardiopulmonary Resuscitation and Emergency Cardiac Care; President, Braslow & Associates, Greenwich, Connecticut.

Richard T. Cook, Jr., M.D., Assistant Professor of Medicine, Division of Emergency Medicine, The Milton S. Hershey Medical Center, The Pennsylvania State University.

I especially want to thank my family, friends and colleagues for their continual support during this book's creation.

TABLE OF CONTENTS

★ **Activities:**

INTRODUCTION

The "S.T.A.R." JUNIOR FIRST AID book is written for children and adults to read together at home, school — anywhere. Each chapter is written using the "S.T.A.R." formula which teaches children to **STOP, THINK, ACT** and **REMEMBER** as they are guided through common situations that require first aid skills. Children can learn to think logically and calmly using this formula and become comfortable with their decisions and abilities to THINK and ACT safely. They should frequently review all the "S.T.A.R." information and practice under the supervision of an adult. By sharing this program with your children, you will enhance their self-esteem and enrich their capabilities. **REMEMBER:** One of these children may someday save a life!

> The information in this book is important for children and parents to know, but it is not intended to be a substitute for official first aid training offered by organizations such as the American Red Cross. Parents are urged to complete an official first aid course.

EMERGENCY HELP

Each first aid topic begins by presenting one or more problem situations that are solved by reading the chapter. Of prime importance in each chapter is a reminder for the children to notify an adult about any unusual incident (whether they tell the adult before, during, or after first aid is given). Sometimes children become frightened if they find themselves alone during emergency situations. Although some children have been taught how and who to call for help, others may not know what to do. Therefore, the "S.T.A.R." JUNIOR FIRST AID book teaches everyone how to reach an adult for support during these unexpected times.

"9-1-1" is the emergency phone number taught in this book. If you live in an area that uses a different emergency phone number, substitute that number for "9-1-1".

HEALTH ALERT !

Blood and other body fluids may spread infection and disease. Protect yourself whenever you give first aid.

You should:

- Wear latex (rubber) gloves whenever you touch the victim's wound, blood or other body fluids . . . or

- Place a barrier, such as a thick bandage or cloth pad, between yourself and the victim's wound to avoid direct contact with the wound . . . and

- Always WASH your hands with soap and warm water after you give first aid. Proper handwashing discourages the spread of germs.

Health awareness and safety precautions are important for everyone to understand. Refer to page 8 for the child's version of these health precautions.

- "S.T.A.R." reminds the children to wash their hands after they give first aid. This is important, whether or not they wore rubber gloves or used a barrier.

- Discuss hygiene with your children. Call the Public Health Department in your city to learn more about the handling of ALL body fluids.

GUIDELINES FOR LEARNING "S.T.A.R."

1. READ

Read this book with your children. Discuss the information in each chapter and define any words that are new to your children. Be sure that they understand them. Refer to the glossary.

2. ROLE PLAY

Follow the "S.T.A.R." formula in each chapter and have your children role play each problem situation. This will allow them to demonstrate new first aid skills that they have learned.

Suggested roles include:

■ One child to act as the victim

■ One child to act as the rescuer who:

- decides whether or not it is safe to be near the victim

- yells for help

- demonstrates the correct skills needed to help the victim

- dials "9-1-1" for help

■ One child to act as the "9-1-1" rescuer who:

- answers the 9-1-1 phone call for help

- asks the caller who he is, where he is, and what is wrong

- gives simple orders such as: "Do not hang up the phone" or "Stay with the hurt person until help comes"

■ One adult to direct the role play

Use imaginary or safe props such as stuffed animals, telephones, bandaids or pots. NEVER use anything dangerous such as matches, knives, electric cords, or electric outlets.

3. REPEAT

Repeating the "S.T.A.R." formula during every role play reinforces important rescue skills which teach children to THINK and ACT safely during an emergency.

4. REMEMBER

Encourage and supervise your children when they practice first aid. Stress the importance of learning to stay safe. Discuss and share ideas about accident prevention with your children. <u>First aid is important to learn but prevention of accidents saves more lives.</u>

ADDITIONAL ACTIVITIES

Aside from reading, discussion, role playing and problem solving, there are four more activities described in the "ACTIVITIES" chapter for your children to do.

- ■ <u>The First Aid Kit</u> is easy to assemble. Follow the "S.T.A.R." directions.

- ■ <u>Test Questions</u> are fill-in-the-blank and multiple choice. Have your children take this test after they have read "S.T.A.R.". Correct the test with them by using the answer key provided.

- ■ <u>The "S.T.A.R." Emergency Card</u> provides a place for your children to list important names and telephone numbers. After you help them with this activity, put the card by your telephone for everyone to use.

- ■ <u>The Certificate of Merit</u> should be awarded to each child who has studied this book.
  (Xerox the certificate if you need more than one copy.)

★ "S.T.A.R." JUNIOR ★ FIRST AID

"S.T.A.R." JUNIOR FIRST AID is a basic first aid book for children which teaches them how to THINK and ACT when accidents happen.

Children care . . . . . Children can help.

WHAT IS AN ACCIDENT ?

An accident is something that happens without warning. Most accidents can be prevented by following simple rules of safety such as:

1. LOOK in all directions before crossing a street.

2. DO NOT play near unsupervised swimming pools.

3. DO NOT play with matches.

4. ALWAYS wear seat belts while riding in a car.

Sometimes accidents happen even when you are trying to be careful.

WHAT DO YOU DO WHEN SOMEONE BECOMES HURT ?

Learn first aid and become a "S.T.A.R.".

WHAT is FIRST AID ?

First aid is help that is given RIGHT AWAY to anyone who gets hurt.

WHO can give FIRST AID ?

Anyone who has been taught first aid can give first aid.

WHEN do you call for help ?

Call for help anytime anyone gets hurt.

HOW do you call for help ?

1. YELL the word "HELP !"

2. If an adult does not come to help you RIGHT AWAY:

DIAL 9-1-1 on the phone.

SAY: "I need help !"
Talk s-l-o-w-l-y.

TELL: WHO you are
WHERE you are
WHAT is wrong

DO NOT hang up the phone after you call for help. The 9-1-1 person may tell you what to do until help comes.

■ "9-1-1" rescue people can be firemen, policemen, ambulance or EMS (Emergency Medical Service) people.

■ If your emergency phone number is NOT 9-1-1, substitute your emergency phone number wherever you see 9-1-1 in this book.

★★

WHO IS A "S.T.A.R." ?

A "S.T.A.R." is someone who shines by his actions. You can become a "S.T.A.R." when you STOP, THINK, ACT, and REMEMBER what to do when an accident happens.

 **S... STOP**

and look at the problem.

■ What happened here ?

■ Stay calm.

★★★★★

 **T... THINK**

Are you in danger ?

■ Is it safe for you to go near the hurt person ?

■ Will you get hurt if you help the hurt person ?

Think about what you must do to help.

★★★★★

 **A... ACT**

YELL for help — whether you are alone or if an adult is nearby. Someone may hear you.

If it is <u>NOT SAFE</u> to help the hurt person:
■ DO NOT go near him.
■ CALL for help RIGHT AWAY.

If it is <u>SAFE</u> to help the hurt person:
■ CALL for help RIGHT AWAY.
■ Use your <u>"S.T.A.R."</u> training.
Give first aid.

★★★★★

 **R... REMEMBER**

Always TELL an adult what has happened.

■ Stay with the hurt person until help comes.

7

REMEMBER . . . Always TELL an adult what has happened.

- Stay with the hurt person until help comes.

- In California all 9-1-1 phone calls, including those from pay phones, are free. If you live in another state, check with your local phone company.

- Write your 9-1-1 phone number on a card and keep it by your phone for everyone to learn.

- When visiting friends or relatives in a different town, ask them to write their emergency phone number on a card for you.

HELP PREVENT THE SPREAD OF GERMS !

Protect yourself whenever you give first aid.

BEFORE YOU TOUCH the hurt person's wound, BLOOD, or other body fluids, you should:

- wear rubber gloves . . . or
- get a thick bandage pad to hold against the wound

REMEMBER:

- Always WASH your hands with soap and warm water after you give first aid. This is IMPORTANT, whether or not you wore rubber gloves or held a bandage pad against the wound.

SANDWICH PLASTIC BAGS

- Rubber gloves give the BEST protection for covering your hands. If you do not have gloves, put each hand inside a plastic bag before you touch the hurt person's wound, BLOOD, or other body fluids.

THE CHOKING PERSON
CONSCIOUS (AWAKE)

NOTE:
The following directions tell how to help someone older than 1 year who is choking on an object. Take a C.P.R. class to learn how to help a baby less than 1 year old, a pregnant woman or any person whose waist your arms cannot reach around.

> Your five year old friend begins to choke on a hotdog that he is eating. He cannot speak or cough hard. What will you do?

STOP   . . . and look at the problem.

■ What happened here ?

THINK   . . . Are you in danger ?

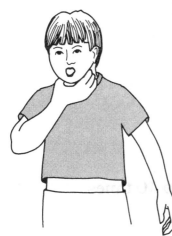

■ Is it safe for you to go near the hurt person ?

■ Will you get hurt if you help the hurt person ?

Think about what you must do to help.

■ Is the person choking on an object such as food, a coin, or part of a toy ?

■ Is he holding his hand near his throat to show that he is choking ?

9

★★★

ACT . . . **How to help SOMEONE OLDER THAN 1 YEAR who is choking on an object:**

1. ASK the person: "Can you talk ? Are you choking ?"

2. If he <u>CAN</u> cry, talk, breathe or cough hard, let him cough the object out <u>by himself</u>.

3. If he <u>CANNOT</u> cry, talk, breathe or cough hard, SAY to him: "I can help you."

4. YELL the word "HELP !" Give ABDOMINAL THRUSTS.

5. Here's how to give ABDOMINAL THRUSTS:

   a. STAND behind the choking person.

   b. REACH your arms around the person's waist.

   c. MAKE a fist with one hand.

HOLD that fist against the person's belly — <u>just above his belly button.</u>

   d. GRAB your fist with your other hand and quickly PULL inward and upward against his belly.

10

6. If an adult does not come to help you RIGHT AWAY or the person is STILL choking:

DIAL 9-1-1 on the phone.

SAY: "I need help !"
Talk s-l-o-w-l-y.

TELL: WHO you are
WHERE you are
WHAT is wrong

DO NOT hang up the phone.

7. REPEAT the abdominal thrusts until the object is coughed out

or

8. STOP giving abdominal thrusts if the person starts to cry, cough hard, talk or breathe.

THE ABDOMINAL THRUSTS HAVE WORKED ! ! !

How to help yourself if you are choking on an object:

■ If you <u>CANNOT</u> cry, talk, breathe or cough hard, give yourself an abdominal thrust.

a. MAKE a FIST with one hand.

b HOLD that FIST against your belly — <u>just above your belly button</u>.

c. GRAB your FIST with your other hand.

d. Quickly PULL inward and upward against your belly.

REMEMBER . . . Always TELL an adult what has happened.

- Always call 9-1-1 RIGHT AWAY even if the abdominal thrust has worked and the object has been cleared from the person's throat.

- Anyone who was given an abdominal thrust must be checked by a doctor RIGHT AWAY.

- Stay with the hurt person until help comes.

- Always WASH your hands with soap and warm water after you give first aid.

- A conscious choking person can become unconscious. Get help FAST !

Give abdominal thrusts to someone older than 1 year who is choking on an object.

DO NOT give abdominal thrusts to:

- a baby younger than 1 year
- a pregnant woman

Always practice giving abdominal thrusts on a big doll or stuffed animal.

NEVER practice on a real person.

- Keep small objects such as coins, candy, parts of toys away from babies or small children.

- Eat slowly and chew your food well before you swallow it.

ADULTS — Please Read

Special attention should be given to this chapter on the choking person. Abdominal thrust is the technique used to help someone older than one year who is choking on an object. Abdominal thrusts can cause injury if not performed properly. They should be PRACTICED ON A BIG DOLL OR STUFFED ANIMAL. NEVER PRACTICE ON A REAL PERSON. The only time a rescuer will use abdominal thrusts on a real person is during a real choking emergency when the person cannot cry, speak, breathe, or cough hard. Abdominal thrusts can also be used to help yourself if you are alone and choking.

Although the abdominal thrust can help a choking person, it may also cause internal injuries — even if performed properly. Therefore, ALL choking victims who are given an abdominal thrust should be examined by a doctor RIGHT AWAY, even if the object has been cleared and the victim seems okay. Follow the directions in this chapter and always call 9-1-1 for help.

DO NOT give abdominal thrusts to a baby younger than 1 year, to a pregnant woman, or to any person whose waist your arms cannot reach around. To learn how to help them, take a C.P.R. class from groups like the American Red Cross or the American Heart Association.

THE UNCONSCIOUS PERSON

> Your father falls down and looks like he is asleep. You cannot wake him up. What will you do?

STOP . . . and look at the problem.

■ What happened here ?

THINK . . . Are you in danger ?

■ Is it safe for you to go near the hurt person ?

■ Will you get hurt if you help the hurt person ?

Think about what you must do to help.

■ Can you wake the person up ?

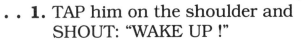

ACT . . .

1. TAP him on the shoulder and SHOUT: "WAKE UP !"

2. If you CANNOT wake him up, YELL the word "HELP !"

3. DO NOT move him.

4. If an adult does not come to help you RIGHT AWAY:

   DIAL 9-1-1 on the phone.

   SAY: "I need help !"
   Talk s-l-o-w-l-y.

   TELL: WHO you are
   WHERE you are
   WHAT is wrong

   DO NOT hang up the phone.

REMEMBER . . . Always TELL an adult what has happened.

- An UNCONSCIOUS person looks like he is asleep but he WILL NOT wake up.

- Stay with the hurt person until help comes.

- Always WASH your hands with soap and warm water after you give first aid.

- Some reasons a person can become unconscious:
  • poisonings • falls
  • electric shock • choking

15

ELECTRIC SHOCK

Your friend grabs a frayed electric cord from the electric outlet. He becomes unconscious. What will you do?

STOP . . . and look at the problem.

■ What happened here ?

THINK . . . Are you in danger ?

■ Is it safe for you to go near the hurt person ?

■ Will you get hurt if you help the hurt person ?

Electric outlets, cords and wires can be DANGEROUS !

■ DO NOT PLAY with them.

■ The electricity in them can give you an ELECTRIC SHOCK !

■ Electricity can flow through wires, wood, metal, people or water.

■ BEWARE — Electricity is invisible. If it touches you, you can become burned or unconscious !

Think about what you must do to help.

ACT . . . **1.** YELL the word "Help !"

2. Keep everyone away from the person who gets an electric shock.

3. DO NOT TOUCH the hurt person ! You can get an electric shock, too !

DO NOT TOUCH HIM !

4. If an adult does not come to help you RIGHT AWAY:

DIAL 9-1-1 on the phone.

SAY: "I need help !"
Talk s-l-o-w-l-y.

TELL: WHO you are
WHERE you are
WHAT is wrong

DO NOT hang up the phone.

REMEMBER . . . Always TELL an adult what has happened.

■ DO NOT TOUCH the hurt person but stay nearby until help comes.

■ DO NOT POKE fingers or metal objects such as keys, nails or forks into an electric outlet.

■ NEVER touch or use an electric cord . . .

  • if you are standing in or near water . . . or

  • if it is FRAYED (looks BROKEN).

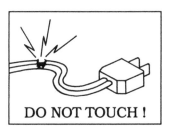

DO NOT TOUCH !

■ STAY AWAY from all loose, broken or sparking electric wires.

■ NEVER play with electric cords and plugs or light bulbs.

■ NEVER yank an electric cord out of an outlet.

■ Call your fire department for more information about electricity and safety.

■ A person can become burned or unconscious from an electric shock. Get help FAST !

FALLS & BROKEN BONES

> Your friend falls down the stairs.
> She cries and says that her arm hurts.
> It looks broken. What will you do?

STOP . . . and look at the problem.

■ What happened here ?

THINK . . . Are you in danger ?

■ Is it safe for you to go near the hurt person ?

■ Will you get hurt if you help the hurt person ?

Think about what you must do to help.

ACT . . . **1.** DO NOT let her get up.

2. DO NOT let anyone move her except a 9-1-1 rescue person.

3. YELL the word "HELP !"

4. If an adult does not come to help you RIGHT AWAY:

DIAL 9-1-1 on the phone.

SAY: "I need help !"
Talk s-l-o-w-l-y.

TELL: WHO you are
WHERE you are
WHAT is wrong

DO NOT hang up the phone.

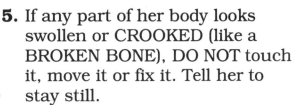

5. If any part of her body looks swollen or CROOKED (like a BROKEN BONE), DO NOT touch it, move it or fix it. Tell her to stay still.

6. If a person becomes sleepy or unconscious after a fall, get help FAST !

REMEMBER . . . Always TELL an adult what has happened.

■ Stay with the hurt person until help comes.

■ Always WASH your hands with soap and warm water after you give first aid.

CLOTHES ON FIRE

> Your friend is playing with matches and his clothes catch on fire. What will you do?

STOP . . . and look at the problem.

- What happened here ?

THINK . . . Are you in danger ?

- Is it safe for you to go near the hurt person ?

- Will you get hurt if you help the hurt person ?

Think about what you must do to help.

ACT . . . **1.** YELL the word "HELP !"
Do not touch the hurt person.

2. Tell him:

- to <u>STOP</u> and NOT to run away.

- to <u>DROP</u> to the ground and cover his face with his hands.

- to <u>ROLL</u> over and over until the fire is out.

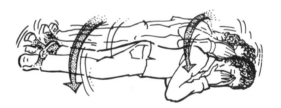

3. If an adult does not come to help you RIGHT AWAY:

DIAL 9-1-1 on the phone.

SAY: "I need help !"
Talk s-l-o-w-l-y.

TELL: WHO you are
WHERE you are
WHAT is wrong

DO NOT hang up the phone.

REMEMBER . . . Always TELL an adult what has happened.

■ DO NOT TOUCH the hurt person but stay nearby until help comes.

■ Stay away from fires.
DO NOT go into a fire to help a hurt person.
Call 9-1-1- for help.

■ Learn more about fire prevention from your fire department.

■ Matches are NOT a toy. If you find them, give them to an adult.

BURNS

> Your friend is cooking soup on the
> stove and the hot soup burns her
> hand. What will you do?

STOP ... and look at the problem.

■ What happened here ?

THINK ... Are you in danger ?

■ Is it safe for you to go near the
hurt person ?

■ Will you get hurt if you help the
hurt person ?

Think about what you must do to
help.

■ How will you stop this burn ?

ACT . . . **1.** YELL the word "HELP !"

2. Tell her to COOL the burn by putting it under COOL running water for 15 minutes.

3. If an adult does not come to help you RIGHT AWAY:

DIAL 9-1-1 on the phone.

SAY: "I need help !"
Talk s-l-o-w-l-y.

TELL: WHO you are
WHERE you are
WHAT is wrong

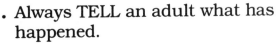

DO NOT hang up the phone.

4. Tell her to COVER the burn with a bandaid or clean cloth pad.

REMEMBER . . . Always TELL an adult what has happened.

■ Always use COOL water to COOL a burn.

■ Stay with the hurt person until help comes.

■ Always WASH your hands with soap and warm water after you give first aid.

■ NEVER put butter on a burn.

■ Beware — hot liquids, too much sun, a lighted match or poisons can burn your skin !

■ Matches are NOT a toy. If you find them, give them to an adult.

POISONINGS

> You find your baby sister under the sink and she is drinking dish detergent. What will you do?

STOP . . . and look at the problem.

■ What happened here ?

THINK . . . Are you in danger ?

■ Is it safe for you to go near the hurt person ?

■ Will you get hurt if you help the hurt person ?

Think about what you must do to help.

■ Poisons hurt fast — Get help Fast !

DO NOT TOUCH !

Many things can become poisons if you put them into your mouth:
• plants
• mushrooms from the yard
• household cleansers
• someone else's medicine
• too much of your own medicine.

ACT   . . . **1.** YELL the word "HELP !"

2. TAKE the poison away from her and SAVE it to show an adult.

3. If an adult does not come to help you RIGHT AWAY:

DIAL 9-1-1 on the phone.

SAY: "I need help !"
          Talk s-l-o-w-l-y.

TELL: WHO you are
          WHERE you are
          WHAT is wrong

DO NOT hang up the phone.

4. DO NOT give her anything to drink or eat unless a 9-1-1 rescue person tells you to do it.

5. WASH your hands if you touched the poison.

REMEMBER . . . Always TELL an adult what has happened.

■ Stay with the hurt person until help comes.

■ Always WASH your hands with soap and warm water after you give first aid.

■ A poisoned person may throw up (vomit). Show the vomit to a 9-1-1 rescue person but DO NOT touch it.

■ A poisoned person may fall asleep or become unconscious. Get help FAST !

■ Keep a small child away from anything that might be a poison.

■ Learn which things are not safe to put into your mouth.

■ For more information about poison prevention, call the Poison Control Center.

Write the phone number of the Poison Control Center on a card.

Keep it by your phone for everyone to learn.

NOTE:
In some cities, call <u>both</u> 9-1-1 and the Poison Control Center for poisoning emergencies.

CUTS, BUMPS AND BLOODY NOSES

Your friend is using a knife to slice an apple and she cuts herself. It starts to bleed. What will you do?

STOP . . . and look at the problem.

- What happened here ?

THINK . . . Are you in danger ?

- Is it safe for you to go near the hurt person ?

- Will you get hurt if you help the hurt person ?

Think about what you must do to help.

- How will you stop the bleeding ?

ACT . . . For **CUTS:**

1. YELL the word "HELP !"

2. Tell her:

■ to COVER the cut with a clean cloth pad or bandaid.

■ to PRESS against the covered cut with her hand until the bleeding stops.

■ to LIFT her arm higher than her heart while pressing against the cut.
(DO NOT lift or move her arm if it looks broken.)

4. If the bleeding does NOT stop or if an adult does not come to help you RIGHT AWAY:

DIAL 9-1-1 on the phone.

SAY: "I need help !"
Talk s-l-o-w-l-y.

TELL: WHO you are
WHERE you are
WHAT is wrong

DO NOT hang up the phone.

5. All cuts should be checked by an adult. Some cuts may need to be checked by a doctor.

Your friend trips over a toy on the floor. He falls and bruises his leg. What will you do?

ACT . . . For **BUMPS & BRUISES:**

1. YELL the word "HELP !"

2. Tell him:

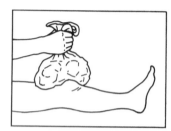

- to SIT DOWN.

- to hold a cold pack against the bump or bruise.

3. Ask an adult to check the bump or bruise.

4. If an adult does not come to help you RIGHT AWAY:

DIAL 9-1-1 on the phone.

SAY: "I need help !"
Talk s-l-o-w-l-y.

TELL: WHO you are
WHERE you are
WHAT is wrong

DO NOT hang up the phone.

5. How to make a cold pack:

- Put some ice cubes inside a clean cloth or use a package of frozen vegetables.

Bumps on the head may be more serious than they look.

Check with your doctor right away.

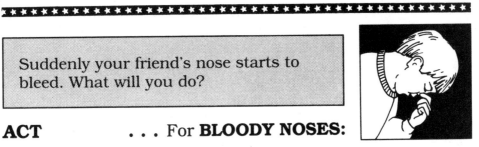

Suddenly your friend's nose starts to bleed. What will you do?

ACT . . . For **BLOODY NOSES:**

1. YELL the word "HELP !"

2. Tell him:

- to SIT DOWN and LEAN FORWARD.

- to PINCH the soft part of his nose without letting go for 10 minutes.

- to BREATHE through his mouth.

3. DO NOT let him blow his nose.

4. If the bleeding does NOT stop and an adult does not come to help RIGHT AWAY:

DIAL 9-1-1 on the phone.

SAY: "I need help !"
Talk s-l-o-w-l-y.

TELL: WHO you are
WHERE you are
WHAT is wrong

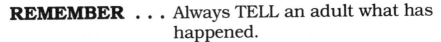

DO NOT hang up the phone.

REMEMBER . . . Always TELL an adult what has happened.

- Stay with the hurt person until help comes.

- Always WASH your hands with soap and warm water after you give first aid.

35

SOMETHING IN THE EYE

You and your friends are at the beach on a windy day. Sand blows into your friend's eyes. What will you do?

STOP   . . . and look at the problem.

■ What happened here ?

THINK   . . . Are you in danger ?

■ Is it safe for you to go near the hurt person ?

■ Will you get hurt if you help the hurt person ?

Think about what you must do to help.

■ Anything such as dirt or sand that gets into the eye can hurt it.

■ How can you take care of his eyes ?

ACT . . . **1.** YELL the word "HELP !"

2. TELL him:

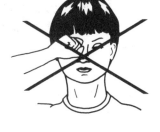

- to SIT DOWN.

- to CLOSE his eyes and NOT to RUB them.

3. If an adult does not come to help you RIGHT AWAY:

DIAL 9-1-1 on the phone.

SAY: "I need help !"
Talk s-l-o-w-l-y.

TELL: WHO you are
WHERE you are
WHAT is wrong

DO NOT hang up the phone.

REMEMBER . . . Always TELL an adult what has happened.

- Stay with the hurt person until help comes.

- Always WASH your hands with soap and warm water after you give first aid.

- EYES are SPECIAL ! NEVER throw anything at anyone.

It may hit them in the eye.

KNOCKED-OUT TOOTH

> You and a friend are playing baseball outside. The ball bounces from her glove and hits her in the mouth, knocking out her front tooth. What will you do ?

STOP . . . and look at the problem.

- What happened here ?

THINK . . . Are you in danger ?

- Is it safe for you to go near the hurt person ?

- Will you get hurt if you help the hurt person ?

Think about what you must do to help.

- How will you stop the bleeding ?

- What will you do with the tooth ?

ACT . . . 1. YELL the word "HELP !"

2. TELL her:

- to SPIT OUT the blood.

- to HOLD the edge of a clean washcloth against the bleeding area.

- to BITE DOWN on the washcloth until the bleeding stops.

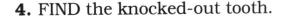

3. If an adult does not come to help you RIGHT AWAY:

DIAL 9-1-1 on the phone.

SAY: "I need help !"

TELL: WHO you are
WHERE you are
WHAT is wrong

DO NOT hang up the phone.

4. FIND the knocked-out tooth.

- ■ DO NOT clean it or scrape it.

- ■ PUT it into a cup of water or milk to take to the dentist.

5. Give her a COLD PACK to hold against her mouth.

REMEMBER . . . Always TELL an adult what has happened.

- ■ Stay with the hurt person until help comes.

- ■ Always WASH your hands with soap and warm water after you give first aid.

- ■ All tooth injuries MUST be checked by a dentist RIGHT AWAY ! Take the tooth with you !

> Injuries to the face may be more serious than they look. Check with your doctor or dentist right away.

"S.T.A.R"
FIRST AID KIT

Here is a very simple first aid kit for you to make. All of the things you need will fit into a small paper bag (lunch bag size). You can carry your kit everywhere.

1 small paper lunch bag
1 small package of tissues
1 small scissors
1 small flashlight
1 whistle
4 small bandaids
1 washcloth
1 roll of 1 inch wide tape
1 pair of rubber gloves

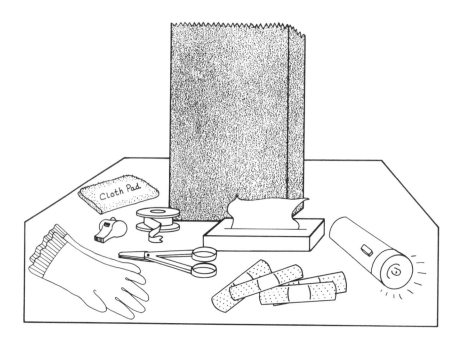

TEST QUESTIONS

Test yourself. Read these problems and use your first aid skills to solve them. Ask an adult to check your answers.

A. Write the answers to these questions:

    1. What do the letters in "S.T.A.R." mean ?

    _____ , _____ , _____ ,_____

    2. What is first aid ?

    _____

B. Draw a star next to the correct answer:

    1. You are heating soup on the stove and your hand gets burned. What do you do ?

        a. Put butter on it.

        b. Turn off the stove and put your hand under COOL running water.

        c. Put your hand under hot water.

    2. Your friend falls down and his arm looks broken. What do you do ?

        a. Try to fix it yourself.

        b. YELL for help and do not move him.

        c. Walk away.

3. Your sister picks a mushroom from the grass in the backyard and starts to eat it. What do you do ?

    a. Taste the mushroom, too.

    b. Never tell an adult what has happened.

    c. Take the mushroom away from her, yell for help. If an adult does not come to help you, dial 9-1-1.

4. How do you help someone who has gotten sand in his eyes ?

    a. Walk away from him.

    b. Tell him to rub his eyes.

    c. Tell him NOT to rub his eyes.

5. Your 7 year old friend is choking on some food. He cannot cry, talk, breathe or cough hard. What do you do ?

    a. Run away.

    b. YELL for help. Give abdominal thrusts to him.

    c. Read a book.

6. Your grandmother fell down and looks like she is asleep. You cannot wake her up. What do you do ?

    a. Do not look at her.

    b. YELL for help. If an adult does not come to help you, dial 9-1-1.

    c. Try to move her.

7. If your clothes catch on fire, what do you do ?

    a. Stop, Drop, and Roll until the fire is out.

    b. Run around in circles.

    c. Do not do anything.

8. Your friend cuts his finger with a sharp pair of scissors. It starts to bleed. What do you do ?

    a. Cover the cut with a clean cloth. Press against it until the bleeding stops.

    b. Laugh at him.

    c. Ask to use the scissors.

9. Suddenly your nose starts to bleed. What do you do ?

    a. Tip your head back and pinch your nose.

    b. Blow your nose.

    c. Sit down, lean forward and pinch your nose closed for 10 minutes.

10. Your dad is in the garage fixing some wiring in the television set. You walk into the garage and find him unconscious. What do you do ?

    a. Touch him and try to wake him up.

    b. DO NOT TOUCH him and dial 9-1-1 for help.

    c. Try to fix the television set by yourself.

11. Your brother's tooth gets knocked out when you are playing baseball. He won't stop crying and he is bleeding from his mouth. What will you do ?

    a. Yell at him because he is crying.

    b. Try to find someone else to play baseball.

    c. Tell him to spit out the blood and to bite down on the clean washcloth that you gave him.

12. Why is it important to wear rubber gloves if you touch the hurt person's bloody wound ?

    a. You need to look like a rescue person.

    b. You need to protect yourself from getting or spreading germs when you give first aid.

    c. You need to keep your hands warm.

13. Do you need to wash your hands after you give first aid ?

    a. Yes, only if you have the time to do it.

    b. Yes, only if they look dirty.

    c. Yes, ALWAYS.

14. Which is the best reason to become a JUNIOR FIRST AID "S.T.A.R." ?

    a. Someday you may want to become a movie star.

    b. You are bored and need to do something.

    c. You want to know how to get help and give first aid during an emergency.

Answer key for "**B**" questions:

1. c	6. b	11. c
2. b	7. a	12. b
3. c	8. a	13. c
4. c	9. c	14. c
5. b	10. b	

★ THE "S.T.A.R." ★ EMERGENCY CARD

YOUR
NAME_____

YOUR
ADDRESS_____
STREET

_____
CITY   STATE/ZIP CODE

YOUR
PHONE NUMBER (_____)_____

★ EMERGENCY PHONE NUMBERS:

POLICE _____

FIRE _____

AMBULANCE _____

POISON CONTROL _____

DOCTOR_____

DENTIST_____

DAD AT WORK_____

MOM AT WORK _____

NEIGHBOR / FRIEND _____

**Keep this card
by your telephone.**

Certificate
of Merit
Awarded to:

Junior First Aid "S.T.A.R."

Cut

★ GLOSSARY ★

"9-1-1" — the emergency phone number used to dial for help; a free phone call

abdominal thrusts — first aid for a choking person who is older than 1 year (Do not use this rescue on a pregnant woman.)

accident — something that happens without warning which may be an emergency

barrier — something that blocks the way or keeps things away from something else

body fluids — liquids from the body, such as blood, vomit, saliva

broken bone — a bone that has been injured and may look crooked or swollen

burn — an injury to the body from heat

choking sign — a signal by the choking person that he needs help

cold pack — a bag of ice cubes or package of frozen vegetables which can be held against a bump or bruise to help reduce swelling and pain

conscious — to be able to feel and think; to look awake

electric outlet — a special place on the wall to plug in an electric cord

electric shock — a dangerous force of energy from electricity that can burn someone or cause him to become unconscious

emergency — something serious that happens without warning which needs fast action

E.M.S. — emergency medical service people such as firemen, policemen and paramedics who rescue hurt people

first aid — help that is given to someone who gets hurt

frayed — looks broken or worn away, such as a damaged electric cord

germs — bacterium or virus ("a bug") which may cause you to become sick

injury — a hurt; harm to a person

lift — to raise up

pinch — to squeeze between the finger and thumb

poisons — a liquid, powder, solid or gas that can cause sickness if it is swallowed, inhaled, or touching the skin

press — to push against

rescue — to save from danger

saliva — watery liquid from the mouth; spit

spit — saliva

"S.T.A.R." — a word formed from the first letters of the words: Stop, Think, Act, Remember which refers to someone who thinks and acts safely during an emergency

"Stop, Drop, and Roll" — instructions for someone whose clothes are on fire

unconscious — looks asleep but will not wake up; not able to think or feel

victim — someone who becomes hurt

vomit — to throw up (something from the stomach)

wound — a cut or other injury to a part of the body

yell — a loud shout

ORDER FORM

To: F.A.C.T.
Sheila Greeley, R.N.
211 Trysail Court
Foster City, CA 94404

Please complete this order form for more copies of **"S.T.A.R." Junior First Aid.**

Name: _____

Firm/Institution: _____

_____Phone:_____

Address:_____

City:_____

State:_____Zip: _____

_____ copies @ $8.95 each =   _____

California residents add 8¼% sales tax   _____

Shipping & handling @ $1.50 per copy   _____

Total amount enclosed $_____

Please make check or money order payable to:
Sheila Greeley

Purchase Order No. _____

Signature: _____

NOTE: Libraries, government, municipal, educational and corporate entities may order by enclosing an official signed purchase order.